D1592339

QUENTIN SKINNER
Thinking about Liberty: An Historian's Approach

15 June 2015, Accademia Nazionale dei Lincei, Palazzo Corsini, Rome

Fondazione
Internazionale Balzan
"Premio"

Accademia Nazionale dei Lincei

akademien der wissenschaften schweiz
académies suisses des sciences
accademie svizzere delle scienze
academias svizras da las scienzas
swiss academies of arts and sciences

THE ANNUAL BALZAN LECTURE

— 7 —

THINKING ABOUT LIBERTY AN HISTORIAN'S APPROACH

by

QUENTIN SKINNER

2006 Balzan Prizewinner

LEO S. OLSCHKI
2016

CASA EDITRICE LEO S. OLSCHKI
Viuzzo del Pozzetto, 8
50126 Firenze
www.olschki.it

ISBN 978 88 222 6460 2

CONTENTS

ALBERTO QUADRIO CURZIO

Vice President of the International Balzan Foundation "Prize";
President of the Accademia Nazionale dei Lincei

FOREWORD

The International Balzan Prize Foundation's Annual Balzan Lecture is in its seventh edition, and this year's, delivered by Quentin Skinner, stands as another testimonial to the Foundation's continued commitment to promoting the most advanced research in science and the humanities. This distinguished lecture series also underlines the ongoing collaboration between the Swiss Academies of Arts and Sciences, the Accademia Nazionale dei Lincei and the Balzan Foundation in their efforts to provide venues for Balzan Prizewinners so that they might present their achievements to the public and share with them issues and findings related to the Balzan Research Projects. Finally, the Annual Balzan Lecture series also recalls the Balzan Foundation's primary aim of fostering communication between the sciences and the humanities at the highest level of international scholarship.

It is a great pleasure to write the foreword to the seventh of these contributions, written by 2006 Balzan Prizewinner Quentin Skinner, as it is not only an occasion for contemporary academic discourse and exchange in all disciplines, but also a way to bring the unparalleled accomplishments of all of the Balzan Prizewinners to the attention of a wider audience.

The lectures cover a wide range of subjects, which reflects the interdisciplinary focus of the Balzan mission and can easily be seen in the short synopsis that follows. The first volume presented the results of Peter and Rosemary Grant's research project involving young academics on the seminal topic of *The Evolution of Darwin's Finches,*

Mockingbirds and Flies. The second lecture by Anthony Grafton, entitled *Humanists with Inky Fingers. The Culture of Correction in Renaissance Europe*, provided a detailed analysis of the impact of these correctors on the meaning of the texts they were working on. The third lecture by Colin Renfrew illustrated the findings from his excavations on the Greek island of Keros in the project *Cognitive Archaeology from Theory to Practice*. Michael Marmot delivered the fourth lecture, *Fair Society, Healthy Lives*, in which he examined the social determinants of health. In 2013, Kurt Lambeck's lecture, entitled *Of Moon and Land, Ice and Strand: Sea Level during Glacial Cycles*, offered a very timely contribution to the debate on the consequences of human impact on the Earth as well as to the very long cycles of changes in the world's physical structure. The sixth lecture, *"Far other worlds, and other seas": Thinking with Literature in the Twenty-First Century*, was delivered by Terence Cave, who analysed selected literary texts to show some of the issues encountered in adopting a cognitive approach to the study of literature, in particular the relation between literary study and cognitive science.

The present lecture, *Thinking about Liberty: An Historian's Approach*, by Quentin Skinner, Barber Beaumont Professor of the Humanities, Queen Mary, University of London and winner of the Balzan Prize in 2006, reflects the direction of his research in recent years, namely, the defence of a theoretical point of view centred on a "neo-Roman", republican idea of freedom, that is to say, freedom from arbitrary domination by others. Operating in the context of the contemporary revival of republicanism, Skinner addresses the classic debate on negative and positive freedom initiated by Isaiah Berlin, and introduces yet another concept of freedom: freedom might be conceived of as independence, which could be a guiding light in the midst of today's ominous political and social dilemmas.

OPENING REMARKS BY ENRICO DECLEVA

President of the International Balzan Foundation "Prize"

I have the honour of opening today's lecture, and I will begin by offering my thanks to the Accademia dei Lincei and its Presidents, Professor Lamberto Maffei and Professor Alberto Quadrio Curzio. I thank you for the opportunity that has been given us to hold the Seventh Annual Balzan Lecture in this very prestigious setting. This annual event, a seminar or *lectio magistralis*, alternates between Italy and Switzerland – in Italy when the awards ceremony takes place in Bern and in Switzerland when it is held in Rome. This year the four Prizewinners will receive their awards from the President of the Swiss Confederation, so the Annual Balzan Lecture is being held in Italy in the context of the long consolidated collaboration between the Balzan Foundation, the Accademia dei Lincei and the Swiss Academies of Arts and Sciences. The idea for and consolidation of this collaboration is due to Alberto Quadrio Curzio, who would probably not be displeased by the fact that his first public appearance in his new role – even if he has not yet officially been bestowed with all the regalia – takes place under the auspices of this tripartite agreement.

Secondly, my most heartfelt thanks go to Professor Quentin Skinner, 2006 Balzan Prize for Political Thought; History and Theory, who accepted the invitation to come to Rome at a time that is not among the most convenient, considering the academic commitments that many of us still have. I must add that Professor Skinner is not only a Balzan Prizewinner, but also a member of the General Prize Committee, and Foreign Member of the Accademia dei Lincei. More importantly, he is a widely recognized scholar (in Italy as well) for his fundamental works on political thought in the modern age, on Machiavelli, but of course not only Machiavelli. I remember that the Balzan Prize was awarded to Professor Skinner on 24 November 2006, in this very room, with this motivation: *for his formulation of a distinctive methodology for the study of the history of ideas, his major contribution to the history of political thought and his acute reflections on the nature of liberty.* Skinner's characteristics will certainly be evident in the lecture – on the concept of liberty, in fact – that we will hear shortly.

In this regard, one of the merits that Professor Skinner is universally recognized for is having re-opened the classic *querelle* on positive and negative liberty, thereby introducing a third and more fitting conception: liberty as independence, as ability to find direction in contemporary political and social dilemma.

Moreover, a natural characteristic of Skinner's scholarly activity and teachings is the extraordinary ability to stimulate discussion and the comparison of diverse intellectual viewpoints and different cultural periods, and this trait has emerged with especially outstanding results in the research project that Professor Skinner carried out with the second half of his 2006 Balzan Prize. As you know, the Balzan Prize is divided into two parts, one awarded unconditionally to the prizewinner and the other to be destined by him/her to one or more research projects that he/she will coordinate. The programme that Professor Skinner has promoted and followed was extremely demanding, and full of in-depth studies and seminars on modern intellectual history and on liberty and the construction of Europe. A remarkable number of junior and senior scholars have been involved, producing various publications and connecting different research centres (Cambridge, London, Fiesole).

The project lasted six years, and has produced two fundamental volumes, *Freedom and the Construction of Europe*, published by Cambridge University Press in 2013. I recall Professor Skinner's coming to Milan that same September to hold the *lectio magistralis* that concludes the announcement of the Balzan Prizewinners.

I am certain that the lecture here in Rome, after the one held in Milan two years ago, will be no less stimulating and full of interesting points. But before giving the floor to Professor Skinner, I will ask Professor Quadrio Curzio to speak.

PRESENTATION OF QUENTIN SKINNER
BY ALBERTO QUADRIO CURZIO

I thank the President of the Balzan Foundation "Prize", Enrico Decleva, for his opening remarks, and for his appropriate and in-depth synthesis of Professor Skinner, an extraordinary personality in modern political thought mainly from an historical perspective. Professor Skinner, as stated by President Decleva, won the Balzan Prize in 2006. The four lines of the motivation of the prize that he read show the General Prize Committee's extraordinary acumen in synthetically describing a figure of outstanding significance in the field of the humanities. Therefore, this Seventh Annual Balzan Lecture represents an important date in itself, and this is also because it falls into the sequence of these extraordinary scholars who, year after year, talk about the main subjects of their research in a spirit which is rigorous but at the same time allows any cultured person to enrich his knowledge.

This sequence of conferences constitutes a point of reference for both the humanities and the natural sciences in that the Balzan Prizewinners, as many of you may know, are the equivalent of Nobel laureates in so far as there is no Nobel for many of the fields that the Balzan Prize has been awarded to. There is no Nobel for history; there is no Nobel for philosophy; there is no Nobel for art history; there is no Nobel for many other subjects that actually represent the foundations of the humanities. I believe that Professor Decleva, like all of us, is very happy that the Balzan Foundation can award this prize to a person who, if there were a Nobel for that particular subject, would certainly have won it or at least deserved to win it.

I say this because beyond any possible merit for having started the Annual Balzan Lecture, it is worth noting that this sequence of brief, concise but very important talks are crucial for the progress of the sciences. If I had to illustrate Professor Skinner's curriculum vitae, it would certainly take more time than I am entitled to. Instead, I would like to use a metaphor that I heard recently from another world-renowned scientist. He said that when presenting famous people one is facilitated by the fact that they need no presentation, and therefore only a few words may suffice for official traditions and politeness. Hence with extreme simplicity I will limit myself to presenting Professor Skinner with the "pin of the Lynxes" that he is entitled to, and that is the pin for members of the Accademia Nazionale dei Lincei.

With this, I entrust him with the task of entertaining us with what will certainly be a wonderful lecture, *Thinking about Liberty: An Historian's Approach*, one of the central themes of Professor Skinner's scientific thought.

Lecture by QUENTIN SKINNER

THINKING ABOUT LIBERTY:
AN HISTORIAN'S APPROACH

I must begin by saying how honoured I feel to have been invited to deliver this year's Balzan Lecture. It's additionally a great honour to be giving the lecture here at the Accademia. I should also like to thank you all most warmly for coming. I have not asked your permission, but I am going to deliver my lecture in English. This is an extraordinary privilege that I'm allowing myself, and it's certainly a privilege that English speakers above all must never take for granted. So *grazie tante, e grazie a tutti*.

I have two principal aims in this lecture, one of which is woven into the other. Basically I want to consider how we might think about the concept of liberty, perhaps the most central concept in our social and political thinking in the Western democracies at the present time. But at the same time, because this is the Balzan Lecture, I want to say something about the Balzan project I directed, a project that the Presidente has already very kindly mentioned in his introductory remarks. I was awarded the Prize in 2006 – in this very room – and I used the prize money to bring together a group of thirty young scholars from across Europe to address questions about the place of civil, religious and political liberty in the formation of modern Europe. We held a series of *convegni* on these topics at the Istituto Universitario Europeo in Firenze between 2008 and 2009. As the Presidente has already noted, the eventual outcome was a two-volume book published by Cambridge University Press in 2013 under the general title *Freedom and the Construction of Europe*. Volume one was called *Religious Freedom and Civil Liberty* and volume two was called *Free Persons and Free States*.

As you can see from these titles, our approach in these *convegni* was historical, and this will likewise be true of my lecture this evening. I've called my lecture "An Historian's Approach", but what I really want to say – and this is the point of the two volumes we published – is that when you examine a topic like that of individual liberty, which has always been a subject of intense ideological debate, and the meaning of which has therefore been contested at all times, you really have no alternative but to approach the topic historically. You cannot hope to arrive at a definition on which everyone might even in principle agree. The concept of liberty has been an object of too much ideological pressure for that. So what you need to do is to follow out the story, and then see what you think about it. That is what we tried to do in the Balzan project, and that is what I shall try much more briefly to do in the remarks that follow.

What historical findings did we report in our *convegni*? We found out very many things – indeed, so many that our two volumes run to nearly a thousand pages. So in talking about our findings I'm going to have to apply a very strong filter. What I have decided to do – with some apology – is to focus on the English language debate. This is not because I think it is the most important one. But it has been very influential, and is certainly worthy of our historical as well as philosophical attention. To which I should add that the English language tradition happens to be the one I chiefly know about; and after many years of giving lectures I've found that it's best to confine myself to what I know about.

What I shall offer you is a genealogy, and genealogies don't really have beginnings, except of course in the Old Testament. But there is a kind of non-arbitrary moment, as it happens, in English language philosophy where it makes good sense to start. We need to begin, I would say, with the first systematic attempt to analyse the relationship of individual to public liberty. This pioneering analysis can be found in perhaps the most important work of political philosophy in the English language, Thomas Hobbes's *Leviathan*, which was first published in 1651. Chapter 21 is entitled "Of the Liberty of Subjects", and it would scarcely be an exaggeration to say that this discussion inaugurated the modern debate.

A further reason for starting with Hobbes is that his account of freedom has proved a very influential one. Really I just need to remind you of it, because as soon as I begin to present his argument you will recognise it. Hobbes's theory is very simple, containing as it does just two components. He proposes that, for an individual to be free – to be free as a citizen of a state – two conditions must be satisfied. There must be power on the part of the individual to act in pursuit of some option (or at least alternative) and there must be no interference with the exercise of that power by any external agent or agencies.

Let me take those two ideas in turn. First, power. Hobbes insists – valuably, I think – that it makes no sense to talk about freedom of action except in relation to your possessing some power to act. If you lack the power to act in some specific way – for example, if you are unable to walk on water – then according to Hobbes it makes no sense to ask if you are free or not free to walk on water. Because you have no such power, he wants to say, the question of freedom does not arise. The reason why this matters is because it suggests that, if some specific freedom has been taken away from you, this must be because you have in some way been disempowered.

Secondly, interference. According to Hobbes, to suffer interference is what it means to be disempowered. So freedom can simply be defined according to Hobbes as absence of interference with the exercise of your powers. But that answer is so simple that it doesn't really get us very far. It turns out that what we really need to understand is the concept of interference. What is to count as an instance of interference? Here Hobbes offers a challenging answer: your freedom is taken away only by acts of bodily interference, that's to say, when an action within your powers is physically prevented or compelled, and where this is the work of some external agent or agency that renders some action on your part impossible to perform.

There, then, is Hobbes's analysis, and as I've said it has been extremely influential, so much so that this strand in my genealogy can be traced down to the present time. If, for example, you look at two of the most ambitious recent treatises in English on the theory of freedom – Ian Carter's *A Measure of Freedom* and Matthew Kramer's *The Quality of Freedom* – you will find that both of them basically endorse something very like Hobbes's account.

You might well think, however, that there is something obviously amiss – or at least strongly counter-intuitive – about Hobbes's analysis. He claims that it is only bodily interference that takes away freedom of action. But notice what this rules out. If it is only your will that has been coerced – if, for example, you obey the law merely because you are more frightened of the consequences of disobedience – then according to Hobbes you are always free to disobey, and if you decide to obey you always obey freely. This is because the State does not enforce the law – or at least not usually – by the exercise of bodily force, but rather by the creation of fear, and hence by coercion of the will. But if, as Hobbes claims, it is only bodily force that takes away freedom of action, it follows that coercion of the will can never limit your power to act freely; it merely helps to determine how you choose and decide to act.

Hobbes offers an example to clarify this doctrine, an example that he adapts from Aristotle. He considers the case of a sea captain who throws his cargo overboard in a storm for fear that the ship may otherwise sink. Aristotle had characterised the action as neither wholly free nor wholly unfree. But Hobbes insists that the action is the product of deliberation, and hence the outcome of a choice, and is therefore wholly free. To which he adds a nasty joke at the expense of those who want to say that the captain cannot be said to have acted willingly. Hobbes retorts that in such circumstances we not only act willingly but *very* willingly. Nothing physically compelled the captain to act as he did. Although he acted under the compulsion of fear, which may be said to have affected his will, this only had the effect of causing him to act in one way rather than another. As Hobbes summarises, "it is therefore the action of one that was free".

There, then, is Hobbes's stark conclusion: coercion of the will and free action are compatible. I now want to turn – continuing with my genealogy – to the political theorists of the next generation. Here we find many writers anxious to insist that Hobbes's argument is much too restrictive. Among these critics, by far the most important was John Locke in his *Two treatises of government*, first published in 1689. Locke agrees that, if I am physically prevented from exercising a power, then of course I have been rendered unfree. But he insists that, if I am coercively prevented – by means of what he describes as the bending of my will – it is likewise true that I do not act freely, or at least not with complete freedom. In paragraph 176 of his *Second Treatise* Locke offers an illustration that he clearly regards as too obvious to be disputed. "Should a Robber break into my House, and with a Dagger at my Throat, make me seal Deeds to convey my

Estate to him, would this give him any Title?". Locke's question is purely rhetorical, because he regards it as self-evident that in such circumstances you have no real choice. So for Locke, by contrast with Hobbes, there are at least two different ways in which freedom of action can be limited: either by physical force, or else by coercion of the will.

But this proposed addition, it might be said, only serves to underline the elegant simplicity of Hobbes's account. Hobbes has no need to invoke the concept that Locke makes central to the analysis, that of coercion of the will. The claim that coercion is the antonym of freedom has subsequently become a central tenet of liberal political philosophy, but the problem is that coercion is not a clear concept at all. How is it to be understood? Locke himself never attempts to define it. He merely offers some examples of the various different ways in which, he thinks, your will can be bent by someone else, focusing on threats, promises and offers in the form of what he calls "sollicitations" or bribes (paragraph 222).

This list, however, suggests that we very much need an analysis. Locke mentions the case of bribes. But do we really want to say that bribes are coercive? Suppose a politician is accused of bribery, and argues in response that the bribe he was offered was so enormous that he had no alternative but to accept it. This will not be accepted as a defence in a court of law. Why not? This is what we next need to explain, and we cannot hope to do so in the absence of an analysis of what it means to be genuinely coerced.

As I say, Locke fails to answer this question, and in fact I cannot find anything like a satisfactory answer in Anglophone legal and political theory until we come to Jeremy Bentham's treatise *On the limits of the penal branch of legislation* in the 1780s. So my genealogy now shifts from the end of the seventeenth to the end of the eighteenth century. Bentham proposes that we should distinguish between two different ways of bending someone's will. On the one hand, you can promise to reward them for compliance with your own will. In this case, if they accept your demand they will be better off, and if they refuse they will be no worse off. But on the other hand, you can promise to penalise them for non-compliance with your will. In this case, if they accept your demand they will be no better off, and if they refuse they will be worse off.

Bentham's proposal is that only the second type of case counts as coercion. As some philosophers have subsequently objected, this is not altogether satisfactory, because it may be possible to offer a coercive reward. But the basic idea still seems to me a helpful one. If it can be shown that compliance leaves you better off, you may be said to have a genuine choice. But if non-compliance has the effect of leaving you worse off, then you can justly claim, if you feel that you must comply, that you have been coerced. For Bentham, the paradigm case of being coerced is accordingly that of being subjected to a threat – provided that the threat itself embodies certain attributes. Specifically, according to Bentham, the threat must be credible, it must be immediate, and it must be serious. But if you are obliged to act under such conditions, then you have been coerced, and your resulting action will not be free, or not entirely free.

Bentham is sympathetic to Hobbes, and his analysis of freedom proceeds along basically Hobbesian lines. But at the same time he complicates Hobbes's account. According to Bentham and many of his utilitarian followers, I am unfree if I am either prevented from acting at will, or else compelled to against my will; and I can be prevented or compelled either by physical force, or else by coercion of the will.

Is this the analysis of freedom that we want? If so, this will be a very short lecture. According to a number of Anglophone political philosophers, something along the lines of Bentham's analysis is indeed what we should endorse. This appears, for example, to be the view of Isaiah Berlin, whose essay *Two concepts of liberty* is perhaps the most influential recent contribution to the Anglophone debate. So this strand in my genealogy can likewise be traced down to the present time.

If we now shift, however, from the eighteenth to the nineteenth century, we find that the Benthamite line of analysis soon came to be seen as unduly simplified. By far the best-known attempt to add further complications is owed to John Stuart Mill in his essay *On Liberty* of 1859. The main complication that Mill wishes to add arises from his belief that there is one element in the genealogy I have so far been tracing that is questionable. This is the assumption that freedom can be taken away only by acts of interference performed by external agents or agencies. One of the questions Mill raises in chapter 3 of his essay is whether freedom is always and necessarily interpersonal in the manner presupposed by this definition. Could it instead be true that the person who takes away your freedom might somehow be yourself?

There is a sense in which this question is an ancient one, and it was powerfully revived in early-modern philosophy by those who wished to argue for a strong distinction between reason and passion. John Locke provides a good example in his *Essay concerning human understanding* of 1690. There he argues that, if your actions are motivated by passion, they will not be wholly free. If you are to act freely, your passions must remain under the control of your reason, which must itself motivate you to act. Otherwise you will merely be passion's slave.

John Stuart Mill is not uninterested in this alleged connection between freedom and reason, but this is not the chief argument he offers for supposing that the self can undermine its own liberty. Rather he follows Alexis de Tocqueville in arguing that, while the yoke of law may have become lighter in their time, the yoke of opinion was becoming more burdensome. The pressure of established *moeurs*, as Tocqueville had maintained, can become so oppressive that we may find ourselves inauthentically internalising the demands of custom in preference to acting according to our own desires. As Mill complains in chapter 3 of *On Liberty*, the outcome is that "the individual, or the family, do not ask themselves – what do I prefer? or, what would suit my character and disposition?". Rather they ask "what is usually done by persons of my station and pecuniary circumstances?". As Mill explains, his worry is not "that they choose what is customary, in preference to what suits their own inclination". It is rather that "it does not occur to them to have any inclination, except for what is customary", and then "the mind itself is bowed to the yoke".

During the next generation, an argument similar to Mill's plea for autonomy and authenticity, but more radical in its premises, began to emerge with the reception of Marxist assumptions in Anglophone political thought. Marx tells us that social being determines consciousness. But if our consciousness is shaped by a capitalist and bourgeois society, then we are liable to find ourselves acting in the light of a false consciousness of what is in our real interests. This strand in my genealogy has likewise come down to our own time in the form of the critique mounted by the Frankfurt School of consumerist societies and the false and alienating values they are said to promote.

By this stage in my genealogy – I have now reached the middle of the nineteenth century – we have encountered a number of strongly contrasting strands of thinking about the constraints on liberty. But there remains one assumption that all the writers I have so far mentioned may be said to share. They all assume that freedom can be defined as absence of interference on some understanding of that term. Towards the end of the nineteenth century, however, this cardinal assumption began to be questioned by a number of writers deeply influenced by Hegel's thought. The Oxford philosopher T. H. Green in particular claimed that, by thinking of the presence of freedom as always marked by an absence of some kind – and specifically by absence of interference – the English liberal tradition had fixed on nothing more than the negative moment in the dialectic of liberty. We ought instead to be asking, according to Green, about the range of specific actions in which our liberty may be said to be most fully manifested and experienced.

It has always been one of the glories of the English liberal tradition to insist that a free person is someone who acts exactly as he or she wishes to act, and that this is the value that most needs to be upheld. The only significant limitation that John Stuart Mill wishes to impose on such exercises of freedom arises from what he calls the harm principle, the principle that the exercise of our unconstrained freedom should not result in harm to others. But for Green this is not enough, because he believes, in effect, that human nature is itself normative, and thus that what serves to mark us out as fully and genuinely free must be our pursuit of a fully human way of life. As Green puts it in his essay *On the Different Meanings of Freedom*, to be free is thus to have realized what you have it in yourself to become, and hence to have fulfilled your true nature by realising the essence of your humanity.

If we reflect for a moment on the broad intellectual traditions we have inherited, we come upon two rival ways of thinking about the sense in which human nature might be said to be normative. We can thereby distinguish two corresponding views about what constitutes our human essence, and hence what would amount to a truly free way of life. Nietzsche may be said to dramatise the contrast in his *Genealogy of Morality*. One vision is classical, and takes the form of the claim that, as Aristotle expresses it, man is the political animal, and is consequently most fully able to realise himself by exercising his talents in the public sphere. Man's essence is thus seen as political. But according to the slave morality that, in Nietzsche's genealogy, is said to have subverted this classical scale of values, the form of service that can be equated with perfect freedom is not service to our community but service to God. Man's essence is instead seen as spiritual.

Although T. H. Green was a Christian, his vision of freedom was fundamentally a classical one. He believes that, as he puts it in his essay on freedom of contract, the forms of action in which our freedom is most conspicuously manifested will be those in which there has been a "liberation of the powers of all men equally for contributions to a common good". To act with full freedom, and hence to realise the essence of our nature, is to exercise one's talents and virtues in the public sphere for the promotion of the public interest.

This strand in the genealogy I am tracing has likewise come down to our own time. Charles Taylor in his *Sources of the Self* similarly argues that freedom must never be seen as a mere "opportunity" concept. To be free is not simply to enjoy opportunities for acting as we choose. Taylor prefers to think of freedom as what he calls an "exercise" concept. To be truly and fully free is to have acted in a certain way – in the way that most fully realises our humanity. But perhaps the most celebrated restatement of this commitment is due to Hannah Arendt in her essay *What is freedom?*. To enjoy our liberty, according to Arendt, is to act "in association with others" in "the political realm", so that there is such a close "interdependence of freedom and politics" that they may even be said to coincide.

I need to pause at this moment, because it would I think be generally agreed, at least by Anglophone political theorists of the present time, that I have now offered as broad a *coup d'oeil* as can be supplied of how the concept of liberty can coherently be defined. But at this point I want to return to the Balzan project I directed and say a further word about it. It was one of our principal findings that something of crucial importance is still missing from the genealogy I have so far traced. So I should like to bring my lecture to a close by speaking about this missing element, thereby uncovering what seems to me the partial and misleading nature of much contemporary discussion about individual liberty.

I can best embark on this part of my argument by returning for a moment to Thomas Hobbes. Hobbes's commentators have frequently noted that freedom, according to Hobbes, amounts to nothing more than absence of physical interference. But they have rarely noted that, when Hobbes proposed this analysis, he was speaking in fiercely polemical terms. He was endeavouring not merely to provide a definition of freedom, but to set aside a rival and completely different definition at the same time. He was so successful in this ideological project that the analysis he was attempting to discredit eventually became largely lost to sight. But it was one of the most important aspirations of those who took part in the Balzan project on "Freedom and the Construction of Europe" to resurrect this different way of thinking about liberty, and I should like to end by adding this missing strand of the genealogy I have been attempting to trace.

For the classic statement (in both senses) of the theory I next wish to examine, we need to turn to the *Digest* of Roman law. (It is a particular pleasure to be talking about the law of Rome in Rome itself.) The *Digest* begins by laying it down, under the rubric *De statu hominis*, that "the fundamental distinction in the law of persons is that all men and women are either free persons or are slaves" (*Summa itaque de iure personarum divisio haec est, quod omnes homines aut liberi sunt aut servi*). The concept of *libertas* is always defined in the *Digest* by contrast with slavery, while slavery is defined as "an institution of the *ius gentium* by which someone is, contrary to nature, subjected to the dominion of someone else" (*Servitus est constitutio iuris gentium, qua quis dominio alieno contra naturam subicitur*). The reason why the *Digest* draws this basic distinction at the outset is that law is concerned only with citizens, and thus with the figure of the *liber homo* or free person by contrast with anyone who is merely a species of property and consequently occupies no place in the law of persons at all.

To grasp the concept of liberty, on this account, what you need to understand is what makes slaves unfree. Here what is crucial is that their lack of freedom is not taken to be signalled by the extent to which they may or may not be forcibly coerced into acting contrary to their will and desires. Citizens who live in extreme poverty may suffer extensive forcible coercion, whereas a slave whose master is wholly benign or generally absent may suffer little in the way of coercion at all. So what is it that assigns to the indigent citizen the precious attribute of being a *liber homo* while denying it to the slave? The *titulus* immediately following *De statu hominis* in the *Digest* supplies the answer. If we wish to understand the concept of servitude, we need to take note of a further distinction within the law of persons: the distinction between those who are, and those who are not, *sui iuris*, capable of acting "as your own man" and hence "in your own right". A slave is one example – the child of a Roman citizen is another – of someone whose lack of freedom arises from the fact that he or she is "subject to the jurisdiction of someone else" and consequently lives *in potestate*, in their power and hence at their mercy in some or all domains of their life. So the lack of freedom suffered by slaves stems from the mere fact of having a *dominus* or master under whose *arbitrium* or will they have no option but to live. You are not a *liber homo* but a slave if you are liable to suffer interference, contrary to your interests, in consequence of your dependence on the arbitrary power of someone else.

This definition of freedom as absence of dependence on arbitrary power has an obvious and important affinity with the liberal theory on which I have so far concentrated. Like the liberal theory, the Roman law conception treats freedom as a negative concept. The presence of freedom is agreed, that is, to be marked by an absence. But there are two radical differences between the liberal and the Roman law accounts. One is that, according to the Roman law theory, the absence that defines the presence of freedom is not absence of interference but absence of background relations of domination and dependence. The other difference is that it is consequently possible, according to Roman law, to be unfree in the absence of any act of interference or even any threat of interference. It is the mere fact of having a master that takes away liberty.

The contention that it is possible to be unfree to act in some particular way even if you face no threat of adverse consequences is one that many exponents of the liberal theory of freedom have taken to be obviously absurd. As the classical utilitarians in particular tried to object, the analysis simply confuses liberty with security. But according to the Roman law theory two responses can be given to this doubt. The first is that, if you live in dependence on the arbitrary power of someone else, then none of your actions will ever be freely undertaken. Whenever you act, your actions will always be in part the consequence of your own will and desires, but at the same time of the silent permission of the person or persons under whose arbitrary power you are condemned to live. You do not even have to be aware of living at the mercy of someone else for this to be your predicament. Many people in ancient Rome were born into slavery, and consequently had no initial appreciation of their state. But from the moment of their birth they were wholly subject to the arbitrary power of someone else, and consequently lacked any power to act autonomously in any domain of their life.

The second response depends on the obvious fact that it will be impossible to live for long in the condition of a slave without becoming aware of your predicament. But as soon as you recognise that you are subject to the will of someone who has power to behave towards you, with impunity, in any way that he or she may choose, you will immediately be liable to embark on a systematic programme of self-censorship in the hope of keeping out of trouble. This will not be because you know that something terrible will happen to you if you fail to behave in a particular way. The horror of slavery is rather that you never know what may be about to happen to you, and will consequently have to do your best to shape and adapt your behaviour in such a way as to minimise the risk that your master will intervene in your life in a detrimental way.

This response stands in one respect in strong contrast to the first one I considered. It is no longer the mere presence of arbitrary power that is taken to have the effect of restricting your freedom of action. Rather your reflections on your predicament are said to give rise to these additional constraints. But in another respect the argument is the same as before. There is no implication, that is, that these further restrictions need be due to any interference on the part of your master, nor even any threat of interference. Your further loss of liberty is taken to be wholly the product of your own self-censorship.

I have said that this way of thinking about individual liberty was so successfully contested and ridiculed by Hobbes and his successors that it largely became lost to sight. But not entirely. One of the main concerns of the contributors to the Balzan project I organised was to focus renewed attention on those who continued to endorse the Roman law conception of the *liber homo* and consequently continued to ask: who may be said, even in the modern world, to live in the manner of slaves?

The answer given by the republican writers of the English revolution in the mid-seventeenth century was that all who live as subjects of monarchs may be said to live as slaves. This is one of the arguments put forward by James Harrington in his *Oceana* of 1656, and even more vehemently by John Milton in his *Ready and Easy Way to Establish a Free Commonwealth* of 1660. All monarchs, they point out, enjoy prerogative rights. But all such powers are *ex hypothesi* discretionary, and hence arbitrary in their nature and use. To live subject to the arbitrary power of another, however, is what it means to live as a slave. So monarchy comes to be seen as the inevitable enemy of liberty.

A further answer, much emphasised when the colonies established by Britain in North America rose in revolt in 1776, was that all who live subject to the sovereignty of a mother country likewise live as slaves. This was one of the arguments put forward by many of the American colonists themselves, as well as by such English supporters of their cause as Joseph Priestly and Richard Price. One of their objections was that the thirteen colonies were being ruled by – and especially taxed in – a Parliament in which they had no representation, with the result that the levels of taxation imposed on them depended entirely on thc will of the British government. This grievance helps to explain why the colonists named their revolutionary Declaration of 1776 a Declaration of Independence. Independence from what? From dependence upon the will of the British government, under which they had no effective control over their own property, and were consequently condemned to living, in that domain of their lives, in the manner of slaves.

A yet further answer came to prominence during the tumultuous years following the outbreak of the French revolution of 1789. Mary Wollstonecraft made an epoch-making contribution to the debate with the publication of her *Vindication of the Rights of Woman* in 1792. Drawing extensively on the vocabulary of slavery, she denounced the fact that, because of their economic dependence, women are obliged to turn themselves into the sort of people that men like, so forcing them to live in the manner of slaves. John Stuart Mill later mounted a remarkably similar argument in his final political work, *The Subjection of Women* of 1869, in which he moved far beyond the liberal arguments on which he had relied a decade before. He too invokes the vocabulary of slavery, arguing in his opening chapter that whereas "the masters of all other slaves rely, for maintaining obedience, on fear", the masters of women have successfully demanded "more than simple obedience", and have "turned the whole force of education to effect their purpose". He adds at the start of chapter 2 that "the wife is the actual bond-servant of her husband: no less so, as far as legal obligation goes, than slaves commonly so called", because "she can do no act whatever but by his permission" and "can acquire no property but for him". He concludes that "the wife's position under the common law of England is worse than that of slaves in the laws of many countries".

Faced with these examples, we may feel inclined to congratulate ourselves on the fact that we now live in democratic societies in which there is full political representation, and in which men and women live in conditions of legal equality. But it would be premature to conclude that contemporary democracies have managed to rid themselves of arbitrary forms of power and the limitations they impose on individual liberty.

One reason for feeling sceptical is that, although we may live in democracies, many undemocratic survivals persist from more hierarchical times. Consider, for example, the extent of the discretionary powers still embedded in the British constitution as a result of the gradual handing over of the royal prerogative to the Executive. Some of these powers stem from the original duty of the crown to guard the boundaries of the realm. They currently include the right to grant and withhold passports, to expel foreign nationals, to prevent them from entering the country, and to judge whether the country is in a state of emergency. Of even greater importance are the powers that stem from the historic right of the crown to regulate relations with other states. These include the right to deploy the armed forces, to ratify the terms of international treaties and, until very recently, the right to declare war and peace. There is no obligation upon the Executive to seek the consent of the people's representatives to exercise any of these powers. They remain outside democratic control, leaving the British people in dependence on the mere will of their Executive for the maintenance of some significant civil rights.

A further reason for fearing that even democratic States may be hostile to the demands of liberty has only recently come to light. We have learned that many western democracies are exercising, without the consent of their citizens, an unparalleled level of surveillance over their daily lives and activities. This has generally been construed as an invasion of privacy, and it is indeed true that, if agents of the State are reading my emails without my consent, then my privacy has certainly been violated. But suppose my knowledge that my private correspondence has ceased to be private prompts me not to say certain things that I might otherwise have said in my emails, or else prompts me to stop sending emails at all. Suppose, in a word, I begin to self-censor, not because I know that something bad will happen to me if I send certain emails, but because I do not know what might happen to me if I were to send them. According to the Roman law understanding of freedom that I have been analysing, this is a clear example of loss of liberty stemming from the fact that I am living in subjection to an arbitrary form of power. By the mechanism of self-censorship, my right to certain forms of freedom of expression has been undermined and taken away.

If we turn from the State to civil society, we find even less reason to feel sanguine about the extent to which the workings of arbitrary power have been successfully eliminated from contemporary democracies. Consider the predicament of workers in de-unionised industries. They live to an increasing degree in subjection to the mere will of their employers, and in the case of industries in which illegal immigrants are widely employed it would be no exaggeration to say that they live at the mercy of their employers when it comes to the settling of wages and benefits. Consider similarly the predicament of the disturbingly large numbers of women who (as recent investigations have shown) not only live in economic dependence on men but suffer domestic violence at their hands. They too are largely condemned to living in many domains of their life in subjection to a purely arbitrary form of power.

With these cautions I bring my genealogy down to the present moment, and thus bring it to an end. I should like to draw to a close by summarising my argument, and to do so by reducing it to a diagrammatic form (see Fig. 1). One reason for doing so is to underline the fact that I have indeed been tracing a genealogy. But my main reason is to indicate as graphically as possible what I take to be

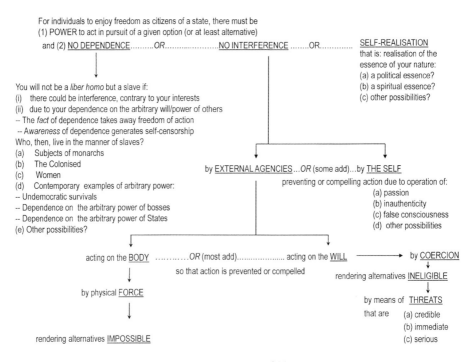

For individuals to enjoy freedom as citizens of a state, there must be
(1) POWER to act in pursuit of a given option (or at least alternative)
and (2) NO DEPENDENCE..........OR......................NO INTERFERENCE ....OR............. SELF-REALISATION
that is: realisation of the
essence of your nature:
(a) a political essence?
(b) a spiritual essence?
(c) other possibilities?

You will not be a *liber homo* but a slave if:
(i) there could be interference, contrary to your interests
(ii) due to your dependence on the arbitrary will/power of others
-- The *fact* of dependence takes away freedom of action
-- *Awareness* of dependence generates self-censorship
Who, then, live in the manner of slaves?
(a)   Subjects of monarchs
(b)   The Colonised
(c)   Women
(d)   Contemporary examples of arbitrary power:
-- Undemocratic survivals
-- Dependence on the arbitrary power of bosses
-- Dependence on the arbitrary power of States
(e) Other possibilities?

by EXTERNAL AGENCIES...*OR* (some add)...by THE SELF
preventing or compelling action due to operation of:
(a) passion
(b) inauthenticity
(c) false consciousness
(d) other possibilities

acting on the BODY ....*OR* (most add)...................... acting on the WILL ———————➤ by COERCION
so that action is prevented or compelled
rendering alternatives INELIGIBLE

by physical FORCE
by means of THREATS
that are   (a) credible
(b) immediate
(c) serious

rendering alternatives IMPOSSIBLE

Fig. 1. A genealogy of liberty.

the point of my remarks. My point is that – to express in Nietzschean terms – genealogy always implies critique. We are frequently told by contemporary political theorists that there is only one coherent way of thinking about liberty, and that it consists in recognising that I am free so long as there is no interference with the exercise of my powers. Contemplating my argument in diagrammatic form, we can see at a glance that this is nothing more than a piece of dogma. I have isolated three distinct strands in the genealogy of modern liberty, each of which is coherent in its own terms, but none of which can be assimilated to the others. We may choose to believe that freedom is absence of interference, but what my diagram shows is that there are other coherent alternatives to be considered. It is not of course for me to say which alternative you should choose. I have spoken as an historian, and my chief concern has simply been to excavate a way of thinking about freedom that has lately been in danger of getting lost. But I freely confess that, as Hobbes puts it in *Leviathan*, "any man that sees what I am doing may easily perceive what I think".

DISCUSSION AND QUESTIONS

Alberto Quadrio Curzio: Many thanks Professor Skinner for this powerful analysis, which presents us with such remarkable problems. Now, if there are questions, I think that if you speak in Italian to Professor Skinner, who understands Italian, he will certainly answer.

Question from the audience: Your opinion about the thinking of Isaiah Berlin and Karl Raimund Popper on liberty in philosophy.

Quentin Skinner: Thank you for introducing the name of Isaiah Berlin, whose writings on freedom have been extraordinarily influential in recent political philosophy, or at least in Anglophone political philosophy. I briefly mentioned him at one point in my lecture, but I am grateful for the chance to place his views about liberty in what I take to be their exact position on the chart I laid out as the culmination of my talk.

Let me first say a word about Berlin and Popper, as you ask. They shared a fear and dislike of totalitarian regimes in which a single ruling ideology is enforced, and in which there are consequently strong constraints on freedom. But these fears carried them in different directions as political philosophers. Popper's basic concern was to contrast what he called open and closed societies. He saw closed societies as those in which traditional forms of behaviour remain largely uncontested, and open societies as those in which pluralism and continuing debate are encouraged. Popper wrote about the place of individual rights and liberties within these allegedly contrasting social systems, but he never focused his main attention on these concepts, whereas the analysis of the concept of liberty became Berlin's principal theme. As I say, Berlin's writings on the subject, mainly published between the 1950s and 1970s, have exercised an enormous influence, so I think it will be right for me to try to answer this part of your question at some length.

Berlin's most famous attempt to elucidate the idea of individual liberty can be found in his Inaugural Lecture as Professor of Political Theory at the University of Oxford, which he published in 1958 as *Two concepts of Liberty*. Here Berlin embraces one particular understanding of liberty while warning us against a rival one. If I may relate his argument to the chart I unfolded in the course of my lecture, I would say that Berlin's preferred concept is the one that occupies the central space in my chart. He believed, that is, that for an individual to enjoy liberty within a civil association, two conditions must be satisfied. There must be power on the part of the individual to act in pursuit of some given option, and there must be no interference with the exercise of that power.

Berlin praises Hobbes's account of freedom in *Leviathan*, and agrees with him that one way in which we can suffer interference is when an external agent makes it physically impossible for us to act as we might otherwise have done. Unlike Hobbes, however, Berlin does not concentrate on this type of case. Rather he emphasises the power of external agents to undermine our freedom by coercing us into acting against our will. He ends up with the claim that liberty should be understood as the absence of either coercive or physical interference. Berlin's central claim is thus that, the wider the area within which I am not interfered with in the exercise of my powers, the greater is my individual liberty.

This is Berlin's preferred version of what he describes as negative liberty – liberty as absence of interference – and he commends it as what he calls the truest and most humane account that can be given of the character of human freedom. But he concedes that there is a rival concept to be investigated, which he calls positive liberty. I must confess that, when he turns to this alternative, his account seems to me very confused. He begins by suggesting that, whereas negative liberty is freedom *from* interference, positive liberty is freedom *to* follow a certain form of life. But there is no distinction here. To possess negative liberty is already to have freedom to do whatever we desire in consequence of being free from interference. Later Berlin suggests instead that the idea of positive liberty is that of being one's own master as opposed to being acted upon by external forces.

But there is still no distinction here. To be free to act in virtue of not being hindered by external forces is, according to Berlin's own analysis, what it means to possess negative liberty.

Eventually, however, Berlin says something more interesting, and certainly more coherent. If I may return to my chart, he finally seems to suggest that the concept of positive liberty refers to the idea of realising the essence of one's nature. It is true that this part of his account is again confused. He begins by arguing that self-mastery consists in overcoming internal obstacles to acting freely. As my chart shows, however, the suggestion that we may need to overcome such psychological constraints if we are to act autonomously can equally well be seen as the overcoming of a form of interference, and thus as an element in one particular theory of negative liberty. The principal claim, however, that Berlin wishes to make about self-mastery proves to be a different and more convincing one. According to those who have wished to give a positive content to the idea of liberty, he suggests, freedom can be equated with self-perfection, with the idea (as Berlin expresses it) of my self at its best. It's true that Berlin doesn't like this way of thinking about liberty, and associates it – although he never clearly explains why – with totalitarian political regimes. But at least he is willing to defend the coherence of this rival account.

As my chart tries to suggest, however, there is a third concept of liberty to be considered. I have described it as the view that, although freedom is a negative concept, the nature of the absence that should be taken to mark the presence of liberty is not absence of interference but absence of dependence. What does Berlin say about that? He was writing at the height of the debate about decolonialisation, and was well aware that many nations and peoples were claiming to be unfree because they were condemned to social or political dependence. Berlin turns at the end of his essay to what he calls the resulting search for status, and he explicitly asks himself if this should be construed as a demand for liberty in some third sense.

Having raised the question, however, Berlin answers that no such concept of liberty can be coherently defended. His objection is that, on this account, there could be absence of liberty without there being any overt act of interference. But to Berlin this seems absurd. It is essential to any idea of freedom, he concludes, that there must be some actual impediment or hindrance to the exercise by an agent of their powers at will. We cannot claim that the mere fact of living in a state of social or political dependence has the effect of restricting our options and thereby limiting our liberty. If you look again at my chart, however, you will see that it is precisely this third concept of liberty that I want to defend and vindicate. I think I have already said more than enough about Isaiah Berlin, but I hope I may be prompted to say something further about this rival view of human freedom in answer to further questions.

Alberto Quadrio Curzio: Professor Brunori, a member of the Accademia dei Lincei, please.

Maurizio Brunori: I have a doubt. It so happened that today I heard on the radio that it is the 800th anniversary of *Magna Carta*. Suppose you have a kingdom where there is only one king – a male – then he is the only person who is free from dependence or interference. There is only one human that is free under those conditions. Is it still sensible to say that freedom exists? In other words, does freedom acquire a significance only when it applies to many people? If there is only one free person, then surely we don't talk about freedom? It doesn't exist anymore.

Quentin Skinner: I am particularly grateful for this question, since it allows me, as I had hoped, to say something more about what I am calling the third concept of liberty, that is, liberty not as absence of interference, and not as self-realisation, but liberty as absence of dependence.

You ask whether any liberty can exist in a kingdom governed by a king with complete freedom to act at will. The answer depends on how you understand the concept of liberty itself. If you think that personal liberty is essentially a matter of not being coercively interfered with in the pursuit of your goals, then there is no reason to fear that such an absolute form of monarchy will be incompatible with the enjoyment of a considerable amount of personal liberty. As Hobbes explicitly insists in *Leviathan*, the fewer impediments you suffer in relation to your choices, the more freedom you possess. But if this is so, then there might be just as much freedom under the sultan in Constantinople as under a self-governing republic such as (in Hobbes's example) that of Lucca. So according to Hobbes and his followers, you would be mistaken to suppose that, if you are living under an absolute monarch, you will no longer possess any freedom at all. That would be their answer to your question.

Suppose, however, you think that what is essential to the idea of freedom is that you should not be dependent on the arbitrary will, and hence the mere goodwill, of anyone else. Then you will indeed think, as you say, that under an absolute monarchy no one can live freely at all. The only person not subject to arbitrary power under such a system will be the monarch himself, so the monarch alone will be free. To cite perhaps the most influential proponent of this idea in modern European political theory, this was emphatically the view espoused by Machiavelli both in his *Principe* and later in his *Discorsi*. The opening chapter of the *Principe* contrasts living under a prince with living in freedom, and the *Discorsi* repeatedly insist that you cannot hope to live in liberty unless you live under a self-governing republican regime.

This is the contention that the modern liberal view of freedom as nothing more than absence of coercive interference has managed to discredit and set aside. But as you can see from my chart, I am anxious to reinstate this rival view in the debate. Admittedly it may seem an obvious exaggeration to say that, under absolute monarchy, no one is able to live and act freely at all. How can the mere fact of living in such a predicament be said to take away your liberty? How can liberty be said to be undermined if there is no actual interference? But the republican writers want you to see that there are answers to these questions that liberal theorists have failed to recognise.

As I indicated in my lecture, the answers given to these questions by early-modern republican writers drew their main inspiration from Roman law. If you look at the beginning of the *Digest*, you find it stated that all men and women are either free or are slaves, and that they are slaves if they are subject to the dominion of anyone else. This in turn is held to yield a definition of individual liberty. If everyone in a civil association is either bond or free, then a *civis* or free citizen must be someone who is not under the dominion of anyone else, but is *sui iuris*, capable of acting in their own right.

The first implication that the republican theorists drew from this analysis was that the mere fact of having a master reduces you to being a slave. As I explained in my lecture, they developed this argument as follows. To act freely is to act according to your will. But if you live in dependence on the will of someone else, then no action of yours will ever be the product simply of your will. It will always be the product both of your will and of the silent permission of the person upon whose will you are dependent. So there can undoubtedly be unfreedom in the absence of coercion or even any threat of it. Next, the republican theorists point out, it is obvious that no one can live for long at the mercy of someone else without coming to recognise that this is their predicament. But as soon as they see that this is so, they will be sure to self-censor in the hope of keeping out of trouble. They will do as much as they can to appease the master under whose power they live. But this is to say, once again, that their liberty will be limited even if there is no actual interference with their choices, or even any threat of it. It will be enough that they know, or think they know, what their master wants in order for them to decide to limit their own freedom of action.

This brings me back to your question. These republican writers want to insist that it is indeed true that, under absolute monarchy, no one can be free except the monarch himself, whose relationship to his subjects, they argue, is that of a master to his slaves. But they would not agree that this is to say that it no longer makes sense to speak of liberty. Rather, they say, what they are showing you is that liberty is intimately connected with forms of government, some of which promote it, while others subvert it completely. A liberal political philosopher like Isaiah Berlin wants to say that liberty can in principle be equally well enjoyed under different forms of government. But the republicans I am citing want to insist that freedom can be enjoyed only under fully self-governing regimes.

You mention *Magna Carta*. But I have to say that, in relation to the argument I am putting forward, it seems to me that the British arguably overestimate its importance. The argument of the republican writers is that, to live freely as a citizen, two conditions must be satisfied. One is that only the laws must rule; there must be no discretionary or arbitrary power. Here *Magna Carta* has some important points to make, especially about such issues as the right not to be arbitrarily arrested and imprisoned. But the republican theorists make a further claim about freedom that *Magna Carta* endorses at no point. This is that not only must the laws alone rule, but you yourself must have a voice in making the laws. If freedom is to be upheld, every citizen must be a legislator. Their reasoning here is as follows. If the law does not reflect your will, then it must reflect the will of someone else. But if that is so, then by living under that law you will be living in dependence on the will of someone else. But to live in such a condition of dependence, they have argued, is what it means to live as a slave. Hence their contention – which of course *Magna Carta* never endorses – that it is possible to live freely if and only if you live under a self-governing form of republican regime.

Alberto Quadrio Curzio: Professor Roncaglia, also a member of our Academy, please.

Alessandro Roncaglia: You've given us a very interesting, multi-faceted idea of freedom in which many aspects interact. To separate out these different aspects, it may be interesting to see whether the forces limiting our freedom change over time. In the past the main force may have been political power in the strict sense. In modern times the limiting forces may be more economic in nature. You also shifted between individuals and the people, all the people. A contemporary example which brings together these two aspects is the present situation of Greece, where economic constraints are certainly relevant in limiting the freedom of the people to freely choose their own way of life.

Quentin Skinner: Many thanks for raising these important observations about the question of liberty in our own time. May I begin by noting that the way in which you frame your question tends to suggest that, when we talk about freedom, we must be referring to specific sources of coercive constraint on the range of actions we are able to undertake. I want to emphasise a different understanding of freedom, according to which it is the presence of background conditions of domination and dependence that play the fundamental role in limiting liberty of action. Nevertheless, I agree with you of course that the operation of coercive force can always limit our options and hence undermine our freedom of action. The republican writers I have been citing do not think of these mechanisms as the most important source of unfreedom. But none of them would deny that, if I try to coerce you into doing something by threatening you with dire consequence if you fail to do it, then I make you less free not to do it. So it is very important, as you say, to ask about the different sources of coercive force that can undermine liberty.

I think you are right that, in some of the earliest discussions of political liberty in modern political philosophy, it was the power of the state – what you call political power in the strict sense – that was treated as the chief enemy of liberty. This is not to say that any of the writers who argued in this fashion were anarchists. They all accepted that the imposition of this kind of coercive force is indispensable if good political order is to be maintained. But insofar as they were writing about the value of liberty, they tended to see the state as the main enemy of liberty, so giving voice to a kind of near-anarchism that continues to underlie a great deal of neo-liberal political philosophy, especially in America, at the present time. I am sure you are also right to say that, in more recent times, governments and citizens have often been more concerned with economic freedoms. The value of loosening the grip of state power on the operation of markets as a means of increasing everyone's range of choices has been emphasised at least since the end of the eighteenth century. We are now living in a period in which restrictions imposed by the use of tariffs have largely been abandoned in favour of freedom of international trade.

To your story I would like to add two further elements. The first, chronologically, is that when the concept of freedom first became a rallying cry in European politics, this happened in the city-republics of *Trecento* Italy. Why do we still see the word *Libertas* inscribed on the gates of the city of Lucca, or on the façade of the Palazzo Vecchio in Firenze? Because these cities wanted freedom in the sense of independence – independence from the Papacy, independence from the Holy Roman Empire, and in consequence the freedom to make their own laws. These were the communities in which the ideal of freedom, understood as absence of dependence, first became a powerful theme in European political discourse. It was from these communities, and from the Roman republican texts that they revived and celebrated, that the republicanism of early-modern Europe emerged, the republicanism of Machiavelli in *Cinquecento* Italy, of John Milton and James Harrington under the short-lived English republic of the mid-seventeenth century, and of the Founding Fathers of the United States at the end of the eighteenth century. The other element I would like to add to the story is that, if we consider how the concept of freedom has been discussed since the nineteenth century, we would want to add the importance of civil society, as opposed to the state, as a potential source of limitations on individual liberty. As I mentioned in my lecture, John Stuart Mill in his essay *On Liberty* of 1859 follows Tocqueville in arguing that the power of custom to impose conformity can be at least as serious an obstacle to living freely as is the coercive force of law.

When you turn, very interestingly, to the case of Greece at the present time, it seems to me that you raise a question that can best be answered by invoking what I am calling the third concept of liberty. One of the most serious difficulties that Alexis Tsipras has faced as Prime Minister is that Greece has become so heavily indebted that it is living in a condition of economic dependence on the European Union, which has in consequence been able in effect to dictate the terms on which Greece is able to remain a member state. These terms contradict the will of a large proportion of the Greek electorate, who have no wish to see such extensive measures of austerity imposed. Greece's condition of dependence has left it with very little freedom to negotiate with the European Union, as a result of which a settlement has been coercively imposed.

Alberto Quadrio Curzio: I have a question, Professor Skinner. One day I met three individuals. The first told me that, to him, religious freedom is freedom. The second told me that political freedom is freedom, and the third that economic freedom is freedom. Each one had the possibility to choose. Which of these three was really free – the first, the second or the third? Or no one perhaps.

Quentin Skinner: I would say first of all that no one can claim to be as free as he or she is entitled to be as a citizen of a western European democracy unless they enjoy complete religious freedom, and at least a considerable measure of economic and political liberty. I think, in other words, that all three of the people you mention will be cheating themselves of important rights and liberties if they equate their enjoyment of liberty with just one of the forms of freedom you enumerate. I would also want to say that the people you mention are mistaken if they suppose that these different forms of freedom are of the same type. The situation is I think more complicated, and I hope it may be helpful if I try to distinguish the different kinds of freedom that may be involved.

Here the first point to make is, I think, that one particular demand for freedom seems to underlie all three of these different visions of what constitutes a free way of life. This demand is what I have called, on my chart, the liberal plea for freedom from interference. Those who call for economic liberty are usually asking for freedom from market regulation of various kinds, and hence for freedom from coercive interference by the state. They want such things as freedom of contract, freedom from tariffs and trade barriers, freedom to dispose of their property at will, and so on. Those who ask for religious freedom are usually asking for toleration, for a willingness on the part of civil society as well as the state to permit them to practise and propagate their faith without being forbidden or intimidated. This is the value underlying Article 9 of the European Convention on Human Rights, according to which the freedom to follow and teach one's religion is an example of a human right. Finally, when we call for political liberty we are usually asking for a list of civic rights to be respected rather than penalised, including freedom of speech, freedom of movement, freedom of assembly and association, freedom to engage in peaceful political protests and so forth.

These calls for liberty are all calls for freedom from interference. But when people ask for economic liberty, and sometimes when they ask for political liberty, what they may instead have in mind is what I have been calling republican liberty. Their complaint, that is, is often that they are being forced to live and act under conditions of dependence and servitude. If you reflect, for example, on the economic relationship between the rich north and the poor south in our present world, the lack of economic freedom suffered by poor countries is often a consequence of their dependence on multi-national corporations and such institutions as the World Bank. The demands that such institutions are capable of imposing in the way of directing investment and controlling employment often seem to reflect the dependent status of the countries with whom they deal. Something similar can be said about some demands for political liberty. Sometimes these are protests not against state interference, but rather against the mere existence of arbitrary forms of power such as the power to arrest and imprison without charge.

Finally, the aspiration for religious and political liberty may sometimes be of a completely different kind, as I tried to indicate in my lecture. Some philosophers argue that freedom is in effect the name of a kind of moral achievement. They want to say that we are fully or truly free only to the extent that we have succeeded in overcoming every obstacle to the realisation of our highest purposes, and have consequently succeeded in realising the essence of our nature. According to this view, to see if someone is free you have to ask them not about the range of possibilities open to them, but rather about how they actually spend their lives.

Within our inherited traditions of thinking about freedom, two main and contrasting views have been taken about how we must spend our lives if we are to count as fully or truly free. I tried to bring out this contrast when I spoke in my lecture about positive liberty. One view, classical in provenance, is that we are essentially political beings. This is the belief summarised by Aristotle in the form of the proposition that man is the *zoon politikon*, the political animal. According to this argument, we realise the essence of our natures most fully when we devote ourselves to public service, to working for the common good. But there is a rival view that historically challenged the classical one. According to this alternative and essentially Christian vision, the essence of our nature is not political but spiritual, and the activities in which we are most fully able to realise our highest purposes are religious in character. This argument preserves the classical paradox that freedom takes the form of service, but argues that the service in question is not service to our community but service to God. This is in effect a plea for freedom from politics, freedom from the demands of civil associations, and the most important institution in which this value came to be expressed was that of the monastic life.

Alberto Quadrio Curzio: So, excluding religious freedom, one day I met a very important person in China, and I told him, "Well, China is going pretty well, but you don't have political freedom". And he answered, "It doesn't matter. We have economic freedom".

Quentin Skinner: It is certainly true that the economic freedom brought to China as a result of Deng Xiaoping's reforms in the 1980s produced remarkable results. China rose to such a height of prosperity in the following decades that hundreds of millions of people were lifted out of extreme poverty for the first time. But I cannot see how it follows from this achievement that political freedom does not matter, which is what your Chinese colleague appears to be saying. Perhaps he meant that China's recent economic success has been so great that all other public issues seem of less significance. But surely the various rights and liberties I listed in the course of answering your previous question remain of great importance whether one's country is poor or rich – freedom of speech, freedom of movement, freedom of assembly, freedom to question our government and so forth. Certainly this is what we feel in Europe, since every one of these freedoms is listed in the European Convention as having the status of a human right. One of the most interesting questions about contemporary China, it seems to me, is whether the ruling Party can hope to continue to promote economic freedom without finding itself confronted by demands for greater political freedom as well.

Alberto Quadrio Curzio: Another question?

Question from the audience: You know you're speaking of a thing so important and so fundamental for everybody which is a sort of doom for a word.

The first point I'm thinking of is that in my generation we used to say that we fought for communism and freedom – *comunismo e libertà*. This is not respected in China, where there is a capitalist state in the sense of a dictatorship of the military-capitalist state.

One question I am asking myself is whether freedom can exist without justice. After the Second World War, there was a very important intellectual movement in Italy, *Giustizia e Libertà*. I think they are twins.

I am also wondering how freedom can be enforced. I am thinking about President Bush when he pretended to 'export freedom' to Iraq by means of weapons of war.

I also wonder, although I am of course opening a multi-faceted cluster of problems here, if you could give us your perspective as an historian on some other aspects of freedom – freedom of the will, freedom of thought.

Quentin Skinner: I am most grateful to you for inviting me to broaden my discussion in these important ways. First, it is good to recall the anti-fascist movement founded by Carlo Rosselli, and to be reminded of his associated writings about the relations between freedom and justice. You speak of these two values as twins, and this seems to me a powerful and attractive thought. I would prefer, however, to express the idea slightly differently, drawing on what seems to me some of the most valuable recent discussions of freedom in Anglophone political philosophy. I am thinking first of the American philosopher John Rawls and his treatise entitled *A Theory of Justice*, first published in 1971. Rawls asked himself how we should conceive the idea of social justice, and he answered that it presupposes equal freedom. So Rawls in effect analyses justice in terms of liberty. I am also thinking of the important work that Philip Pettit has recently been publishing about what I have been calling the republican theory of liberty, most notably his book of 1997 entitled *Republicanism*. By contrast with Rawls, who thinks of freedom essentially as a matter of minimising unjust interference, Pettit wishes to insist that I am fully free if and only if I am robustly protected against any such acts of interference by way of being independent of arbitrary domination by others. It is Pettit's claim that, if we could achieve a society in which such arbitrary powers are eliminated, so that everyone enjoys equal freedom in the sense of independence from domination, then we would at the same time have achieved a society in which there is real social justice. On this account, freedom and justice are in effect two different names for the same core value.

Next you ask how freedom can be enforced. This is not a question I have discussed, but there is certainly a paradox lurking here that deserves to be examined. We all agree, I assume, that the minimising of unjust coercion is one means of maintaining and increasing civil liberty. But the chief means we use to uphold freedom in the face of such coercion is to apply the force of law to prevent the exercise of such unjust force. However, the basic way in which the law operates is by inhibiting us from acting in certain ways by making us more frightened of the consequences of acting than of not acting. But this is to say that we cannot have liberty without coercion. I have said that this is a paradox. But if it is, then it seems to me one of the paradoxes that we cannot hope to avoid in political philosophy and politics alike.

Finally you ask me to widen my focus still further by saying something about freedom of thought, and about freedom of the will. You are of course right to say that my focus has been a relatively narrow one. I have been concerned exclusively with questions about freedom of action and what it might mean to say that someone's freedom of action has been limited. But this is already a huge question, and I fear that I do not have the time or the talent to expand it further in the directions you ask. But let me just make two quick points.

First, about freedom of thought. There has been an important tradition – again, a largely Christian one – which has wanted to insist that this purely internal kind of freedom is the most important form of human liberty. The most celebrated affirmation of this value can be found in Boethius's *Consolation of Philosophy*, written in the early sixth century. Boethius composed the work while in prison under sentence of death – a sentence that was duly carried out. The figure of the Lady Philosophy appears to him in a vision, and the consolation that she offers him is that, even in his grave predicament, he can comfort himself with the thought that he remains entirely free. This is because he still enjoys freedom of thought, which the Lady Philosophy takes to be the most important freedom of all, since its enjoyment remains entirely under our own control at all times. No doubt this is an exaggeration, but it reminds us how much we value the freedom to think our own thoughts as well as the freedom to act as we choose.

Next, and lastly, a thought about freedom of the will. I have not said anything explicit about the metaphysics of freedom. But everything I have said about freedom of action presupposes that, when we act, we can do either this or that. So have I not presupposed freedom of the will? Not necessarily, because there can surely be free actions even if the will is not free. If free action is simply unconstrained action, or action undertaken independently of the will of anyone else, then my will may be wholly determined and my actions may nevertheless be free, simply because they are not restricted in either of these ways.

Alberto Quadrio Curzio: So, many thanks indeed to Professor Skinner for this thoughtful lecture, and for his answers to our questions. To conclude our meeting tonight, I would like to give you a book which is about freedom of scientific research. It's a study of Galileo, and so might give you another look at freedom of thought.

Quentin Skinner: How wonderful. Thank you very much.

Alberto Quadrio Curzio: Thank you very much.

2015 Annual Balzan Lecture, Accademia Nazionale dei Lincei, Rome. Above: Palazzo Corsini, headquarters of the Accademia. Below: from the left, Balzan Distinguished Lecturer Quentin Skinner; President of the Accademia dei Lincei Alberto Quadrio Curzio; International Balzan Foundation "Prize" President Enrico Decleva.

2015 Annual Balzan Lecture, Accademia Nazionale dei Lincei, Rome. Above: Gardens of the Villa Farnesina, Quentin Skinner and other guests take a guided tour. Below: the Villa Farnesina.

2015 Annual Balzan Lecture, Accademia Nazionale dei Lincei, Rome. Above: Balzan Distinguished Lecturer Quentin Skinner. Below: Quentin Skinner lectures to an attentive audience.

2015 Annual Balzan Lecture, Accademia Nazionale dei Lincei, Rome. Above: a member of the audience during the Discussion and Questions session. Below: Balzan Distinguished Lecturer Quentin Skinner accepts a book on Galileo Galilei from Accademia dei Lincei President Alberto Quadrio Curzio while International Balzan Foundation "Prize" President Enrico Decleva looks on.

QUENTIN SKINNER

BIOGRAPHICAL AND BIBLIOGRAPHICAL DATA

Barber Beaumont Professor of the Humanities at Queen Mary, University of London, Quentin Skinner is one of today's most eminent and influential intellectual historians. In the late 1960s and early 1970s, he elaborated a theoretical and philosophical point of view centred on the nature of political discourse understood as a series of linguistic acts, and on the historian's task of interpreting texts in contexts.

Thanks to the methodological tools made available by his approach, Skinner has been able to develop an impressive range of historical research dedicated to a new, original interpretation of the genesis of political categories and points of view during the medieval and early modern periods in Europe, focusing above all on the genesis of the modern idea of the state. His fundamental contribution in this area remains his monumental two-volume study entitled *The Foundations of Modern Political Thought*, which came out in 1978. This has long been regarded as a classic text, and in 1996 it was included by the *Times Literary Supplement* in its list of the hundred most influential books published since World War II.

Skinner published his *summa* in 2002: *Visions of Politics*. The first volume, *Regarding Method*, is a collection of his contributions to the theory of interpretation. The second, *Renaissance Virtues*, is dedicated to the historical reconstruction of the phenomenon of republicanism as a theory of freedom and good government between the thirteenth and sixteenth century. The third, *Hobbes and Civil Science*, is an innovative interpretation of the political thought of this major English philosopher, an interpretation that Skinner has since carried further in his more recent book *Hobbes and Republican Liberty* (2008).

In recent years, following his *Liberty before Liberalism* (1998), Skinner has been involved in the defence of a theoretical point of view centred on a "neo-Roman" idea of freedom, understood in the republican sense of freedom from arbitrary domination by others. Against the background of the contemporary revival of republicanism, Skinner re-opens the classic *querelle* on negative and positive freedom inaugurated in Isaiah Berlin's famous study by introducing a third concept of freedom as independence, a concept that can help to orient us in some of our contemporary political and social dilemmas.

Skinner's other long-standing research interest has been in classical rhetoric and its revival in the Renaissance. He began by studying the political uses of rhetoric in the city-states of the early Italian Renaissance. Later, in *Reason and Rhetoric in the Philosophy of Hobbes* (1996), he examined the discrediting of rhetoric by the so-called new philosophy in the course of the seventeenth century. More recently he has focused on the heyday of English rhetorical education in the sixteenth century and traced its influence on the rise of the drama in his latest book, *Forensic Shakespeare* (2014).

During the past decades, Skinner's untiring efforts in carrying out research and training scholars in the field of intellectual history have constantly been accompanied by extensive editorial work, including the editorship of two series for the Cambridge University Press: *Ideas in Context*, in which over 100 monographs have been published, and *Cambridge Texts in the History of Political Thought*, in which more than 120 volumes have so far appeared. His intellectual work has consolidated a truly new paradigm in the field of the history and theory of political thought.

Quentin Skinner's membership of learned societies is extensive: he is Corresponding Fellow of the Österreichische Academie der Wissenschaften (2009), Foreign Member of the Accademia Nazionale dei Lincei (2007) and the American Philosophical Society (1997), Honorary Member of the Royal Irish Academy (1999), Foreign Honorary Member of the American Academy of Arts and Sciences (1986), Fellow of the Royal Society of Arts (1996), the Academia Europea (1989), the British Academy (1981), and the Royal Historical Society (1971). His scholarly contributions have been recognized by numerous Honorary Degrees and Fellowships from universities all over the world.

The following institutions have recognized Skinner's achievements by granting him honorary degrees: the Universities of Copenhagen (2014) and Oslo (2011), the Universidad Adolfo Ibáñez in Santiago (2009), the Universities of Aberdeen and Athens (both in 2007), the University of St. Andrews and Harvard University (both in 2005), the Katholieke Universiteit Leuven (2004), the Universities of Oxford (2000), Helsinki (1997), East Anglia and Chicago (both in 1992).

A prolific author, his bibliography includes over one hundred articles in addition to his books. His scholarship is available in twenty languages (Chinese, Czech, Dutch, Finnish, French, German, Greek, Hebrew, Hungarian, Indonesian, Italian, Japanese, Korean, Polish, Portuguese, Romanian, Russian, Spanish, Swedish and Turkish). A selection of his most important publications follows:

– *The Foundations of Modern Political Thought, Vol. I: The Renaissance*, Cambridge, Cambridge University Press, 1978. Translated into Chinese, French, Italian, Korean, Portuguese, Spanish.

– *The Foundations of Modern Political Thought, Vol. II: The Age of Reformation*, Cambridge, Cambridge University Press, 1978. Translated into Chinese, French, Italian, Portuguese, Spanish.

– *Machiavelli*, Oxford, Oxford University Press, 1981. Translated into Chinese, Czech, French, German, Greek, Hebrew, Hungarian, Indonesian, Italian, Japanese, Korean, Portuguese, Romanian, Spanish, Swedish.

– *Philosophy in History* (ed. with Richard Rorty and Jerome B. Schneewind), Cambridge, Cambridge University Press, 1984.

– *The Return of Grand Theory in the Human Sciences* (ed.), Cambridge, Cambridge University Press, 1985. Translated into Greek, Japanese, Polish, Portuguese, Spanish, Turkish.

– *The Cambridge History of Renaissance Philosophy* (ed. with Charles B. Schmitt), Cambridge, Cambridge University Press, 1988.

– *Machiavelli, The Prince* (ed., translation by Russell Price), Cambridge, Cambridge University Press, 1988.

– *Meaning and Context: Quentin Skinner and his Critics* (ed. by James Tully), Cambridge, Polity Press, 1988; Princeton, Princeton University Press, 1989. Translated into Chinese, Japanese, Korean.

- *Machiavelli and Republicanism* (ed. with Gisela Bocks and Maurizio Viroli), Cambridge, Cambridge University Press, 1990.
- *Political Discourse in Early-modern Britain* (ed. with Nicholas Phillipson), Cambridge, Cambridge University Press, 1993.
- *Milton and Republicanism* (ed. with David Armitage and Armand Himy), Cambridge, Cambridge University Press, 1995.
- *Reason and Rhetoric in the Philosophy of Hobbes*, Cambridge, Cambridge University Press, 1996. Translated into Chinese, Portuguese.
- *Liberty before Liberalism*, Cambridge, Cambridge University Press, 1998. Translated into Chinese, French, Greek, Italian, Portuguese, Russian, Spanish.
- *Visions of Politics, Vol. I: Regarding Method*, Cambridge, Cambridge University Press, 2002. Translated into Greek, Italian, Portuguese.
- *Visions of Politics, Vol. II: Renaissance Virtues*, Cambridge, Cambridge University Press, 2002.
- *Visions of Politics, Vol. III: Hobbes and Civil Science*, Cambridge, Cambridge University Press, 2002.
- *Republicanism: A Shared European Heritage, Vol. I: Republicanism and Constitutionalism in Early Modern Europe* (ed. with Martin Van Gelderen), Cambridge, Cambridge University Press, 2002.
- *Republicanism: A Shared European Heritage, Vol. II: The Values of Republicanism in Early Modern Europe* (ed. with Martin Van Gelderen), Cambridge, Cambridge University Press, 2002.
- "A Third Concept of Liberty", *Proceedings of the British Academy*, 117 (2002), pp. 237-268. Translated into Chinese, Finnish, French, Spanish.
- *States and Citizens: History, Theory, Prospects* (ed. with Bo Stråth), Cambridge, Cambridge University Press, 2003.
- *L'artiste en philosophie politique*, Paris, Éditions de Seuil, 2003.
- *Thomas Hobbes: Writings on Common Law and Hereditary Right* (The Clarendon Edition of the Works of Thomas Hobbes, Volume XI, ed. with Alan Cromartie), Oxford, Clarendon Press, 2005.
- *Hobbes and Republican Liberty*, Cambridge, Cambridge University Press, 2008. Translated into Chinese, French, German, Portuguese, and Spanish. Japanese and Romanian translations forthcoming.

– *Vilkårlig Makt: Essays om Politisk Frihet*, Oslo, Forlaget Res Publica, 2009.

– *Sovereignty in Fragments: The Past, Present and Future of a Contested Concept* (co-editor and contributor), Cambridge, Cambridge University Press, 2010.

– *La verité et l'historien* (ed. Christopher Hamel), Paris, Éditions EHESS, 2010.

– *Families and States in Western Europe* (ed.), Cambridge, Cambridge University Press, 2011.

– *Uma Genealogia do Estado Moderno*, Lisbon, Imprensa de Ciências Socials, 2011.

– *Die drei Körper des Staates*, Göttingen, Wallstein, 2012.

– *Freedom and the Construction of Europe* (co-editor and contributor), two volumes, Cambridge, Cambridge University Press, 2013.

– *Forensic Shakespeare*, Oxford, Oxford University Press, 2014.

BALZAN-SKINNER ANNUAL LECTURES
AND INTERNATIONAL CONFERENCES

Adviser for the Balzan General Prize Committee: Salvatore Veca

Quentin Skinner used the second half of his 2006 Balzan Prize for Political Thought; History and Theory on a twofold research project consisting of Annual Lectures and International Conferences.

The annual lectures were delivered at the University of Cambridge under the joint auspices of the Faculty of History and the Centre for Research in the Arts, Social Sciences and Humanities (CRASSH). The Managers of CRASSH, who sat on the Appointments Committee for the Lectureship, agreed that each lecturer should also be made a Fellow at CRASSH during the academic term in which the lecture and accompanying conference took place, thereby providing a period of residence at Cambridge and the opportunity to make use of the full range of its outstanding facilities for research.

The regulations for the series required the lectureship to be restricted to younger researchers (less than 10 years into their careers after completion of the PhD). Each lecture had to be delivered on a topic in Modern Intellectual History (1500 to the present day). A one-day Conference was associated with each one, and other younger researchers in the relevant field were invited. An Appointments Committee ensured that the lectureship was equally open and hospitable to researchers working in all idioms and traditions of intellectual history.

The first lecture, *Normativity of Nature*, was delivered by Dr. Hannah Dawson of the University of Edinburgh in September 2010; the second, *Radical Translation: Analytic Philosophy in America*, by Dr. Joel Isaac of Queen Mary, University of London in May 2011. The third lecture, *John Locke and the Fable of Liberalism*, was delivered in October 2012 by Dr. Timothy Stanton of the University of York. Dr. Gabriel Paquette, Assistant Professor of History at Johns Hopkins

University, delivered the fourth lecture, *Romantic Liberalism in Southern Europe, c. 1820-1850*, in April 2013. The fifth was delivered by Dr. Karuna Mantena Associate Professor of Political Science at Yale University in May 2014 under the title *Gandhi's Realism: Means and Ends in Politics*. Dr. Anna Becker, University of Basel, gave the sixth lecture on *Gender in the History of Early Modern Political Thought* in May 2015, and Dr. Teresa Bejan University of Oxford, *Acknowledging Equality: respect and contempt in seventeenth-century English political thought*, will give the final lecture in April 2016. Full details of the lectures and conferences can be found on the CRASSH website, www.crassh.cam.ac.uk/programmes/balzan-skinner-fellowship.

The series of four international conferences under the general title *Freedom and the Construction of Europe* was held between July 2008 and September 2009 at the Conference Centre of the European University Institute (EUI) at San Domenico di Fiesole (Florence). As the result of an international advertisement, over a hundred applications were received from young scholars wishing to join the core group. After dossiers and references had been read, twenty-two names were selected. The first conference (3-5 July 2008) was concerned with *Religious Freedom and Civil Liberty*. The second followed on 25-27 September 2008, and was entitled *Liberty and Liberties in Legal and Constitutional Thought*. The third and fourth conferences were on the topics *The Freedom of Individuals* (2-4 July 2009) and *European Freedom and its Boundaries* (24-26 September 2009). For complete details on the conferences, consult the project website at apps.eui.eu/Personal/Projects/FreedomProject/Abouttheproject.shtml.

A major publication has come out of the EUI Conferences. Before they were held, a steering committee was formed to work out the topics to be covered at each individual conference, and to make plans for the possible publication of the conference proceedings as a book. Members of the steering committee included the Prizewinner, Quentin Skinner, together with the Professor of Early Modern History at the European University Institute, Professor Martin van Gelderen, who acted as host to the conferences, and Mr. Richard Fisher, head of Humanities and Social Science publishing at the Cambridge University Press. The resulting work is the two-volume book edited by Skinner and Van Gelderen, *Freedom and the Construction of Europe* (Cambridge University Press, 2013).

A NOTE ON THE BALZAN RESEARCH PROJECTS
BY SALVATORE VECA

Chairman of the International Balzan Foundation's General Prize Committee;
Professor of Political Philosophy at the Istituto Universitario di Studi Superiori
(IUSS), Pavia

The Balzan Research Projects are an integral part of the Balzan Prize and are the most important element that distinguishes it from other international awards. The projects are a concrete manifestation of the central aims of the Balzan Foundation as defined by Lina Balzan: to promote culture, the sciences and the most meritorious initiatives in the cause of humanity and peace among peoples throughout the world. Since 2001, half of each annual Balzan Prize must be set aside to support a research project developed by the Prizewinner and approved by the Balzan General Prize Committee. The structure of each research project is designed by the Prizewinner, who is responsible for its management at an academic institution designated by him or her. The Balzan General Prize Committee delegates one or more of its members to advise and assist Prizewinners in the definition and implementation of their projects. Another outstanding characteristic of these projects and hence of the Balzan Prize in general is that they are intended to give young researchers an opportunity to make an impact at the beginning of their careers.

The vast range and sheer diversity of the projects undertaken to date is remarkable, and all academic disciplines – from the most traditional, like classical archaeology, to the most futuristic, like quantum information processing and communication – are present among the list of projects that have been carried out or that are still in progress. Among these many different fields of research, new and emerging ones are included, as the subjects of the Prizes vary from year to year. This is another unique feature of the Balzan Prize: it ensures constant innovation in science and the humanities. Significant cutting edge research has emanated from these endeavours, with Balzan

Prizes supporting the purchase of laboratory equipment, financing expeditions and publishing major academic works. The variety and quality of this output has also resulted in the establishment of a singular library at the headquarters of the Balzan Prize Foundation in Milan, which is available to interested academics and researchers.

The total amount to date allocated to over fifty Balzan Research Projects is over 26 million Swiss francs. A significant number of academic institutions and individual researchers worldwide have been involved in these research projects, from countries including Australia, Austria, Canada, France, Germany, Greece, Italy, Japan, Poland, Russia, Switzerland, the Netherlands, the UK and the USA. Over five hundred researchers and administrators have been involved, representing an input from many other countries including China, Finland, India, Iran, Romania, Ukraine, Ireland and Poland.

Our Prizewinners welcome this innovative, distinguishing characteristic of the Balzan Prize. They have acknowledged the projects as a celebration of the values of scholarship, as recognition of different disciplines, and as a challenge to embark on new research. Most importantly, they have emphasized the opportunity the Balzan Foundation has given them to help a new generation of scholars and thereby build the future.

PROFILES

The International Balzan Foundation

The *International Balzan Foundation "Prize"* aims to promote, throughout the world, culture, science, and the most meritorious initiatives in the cause of humanity, peace and fraternity among peoples, regardless of nationality, race or creed. This aim is attained through the annual award of prizes in two general academic categories: literature, the moral sciences and the arts; medicine and the physical, mathematical and natural sciences. Specific subjects for the awarding of Prizes are chosen on an annual basis.

Nominations for these prizes are received at the Foundation's request from the world's leading academic institutions. Candidates are selected by the *General Prize Committee*, composed of eminent European scholars and scientists. Prizewinners must allocate half of the Prize to research work, preferably involving young researchers.

At intervals of not less than three years, the Balzan Foundation also awards a prize of varying amounts for Humanity, Peace and Fraternity among Peoples.

The *International Balzan Foundation "Prize"* attains its financial means from the *International Balzan Foundation "Fund"* which administers Eugenio Balzan's estate.

The Accademia Nazionale dei Lincei

The *Accademia Nazionale dei Lincei*, founded in 1603 by the Roman-Umbrian aristocrat Federico Cesi and three other young scholars, Anastasio De Filiis, Johannes Eck and Francesco Stelluti, is the oldest scientific academy in the world. It promotes academic excellence through its Fellows whose earliest members included, among many other renowned names, Galileo Galilei.

The Academy's mission is "to promote, coordinate, integrate and disseminate scientific knowledge in its highest expressions in the context of cultural unity and universality".

The activities of the Academy are carried out according to two guiding principles that complement one another: to enrich academic knowledge and disseminate the fruits of this. To this end, the *Accademia Nazionale dei Lincei* organises national and international conferences, meetings and seminars, and encourages academic cooperation and exchange between scientists and scholars at the national and international level. The Academy promotes research activities and missions, confers awards and grants, publishes the reports of its own sessions and the notes and records presented therein, as well as the proceedings of its conferences, meetings and seminars.

The Academy further provides – either upon request or on its own initiative – advice to public institutions and drafts relevant reports when appropriate. Since 1992, the Academy has served as an official adviser to the President of the Italian Republic in relation to scholarly and scientific matters.

THE SWISS ACADEMIES OF ARTS AND SCIENCES

The Association of the *Swiss Academies of Arts and Sciences* includes the Swiss Academy of Sciences (SCNAT), the Swiss Academy of Humanities and Social Sciences (SAHS), the Swiss Academy of Medical Sciences (SAMS), and the Swiss Academy of Engineering Sciences (SATW) as well as the two Centres for Excellence TA-SWISS and Science et Cité. Their collaboration is focused on methods of anticipating future trends, ethics and the dialogue between science, the arts and society. It is the aim of the *Swiss Academies of Arts and Sciences* to develop an equal dialogue between academia and society and to advise Government on scientifically based, socially relevant questions. The academies stand for an open and pluralistic understanding of science and the arts. Over the long-term, they mutually commit to resolving interdisciplinary questions in the following areas:

– They offer knowledge and expertise in relation to socially relevant subjects in the fields of Education, Research and Technology.
– They adhere to the concept of ethically-based responsibility in gaining and applying scientific and humanistic knowledge.
– They build bridges between Academia, Government and Society.

AGREEMENTS ON COLLABORATION BETWEEN
THE INTERNATIONAL BALZAN FOUNDATION "PRIZE",
THE SWISS ACADEMIES OF ARTS AND SCIENCES
AND THE ACCADEMIA NAZIONALE DEI LINCEI

(Hereafter referred to as the 'Balzan', the 'Swiss Academies' and the 'Lincei', respectively)

The main points of the agreements between the Balzan, the Swiss Academies and the Lincei are the following:

1) The promotion of the Balzan Prize and the presentation of the Prizewinners through the academies' channels of communication, in Italy and Switzerland as well as abroad. By virtue of the relations of the Swiss Academies and the Lincei with academies of other countries and with international academic organizations, they will contribute to more widespread circulation of news related to the Balzan;

2) On the occasion of the Awards ceremony of the Balzan Prize, held on alternating years in Berne and Rome, each academy will contribute to the academic organization of an interdisciplinary Forum, in the course of which the Prizewinners of that year will present their academic work and discuss it with other academics proposed by the academies. Furthermore, in the years when the ceremony is held in Rome, one of the Prizewinners will give the Annual Balzan Lecture in Switzerland, and when the ceremony is held in Berne, the Annual Balzan Lecture will be organized at the headquarters of the Lincei in Rome;

3) The academies will contribute to a series of publications in English (ideally with summaries in Italian, German and French), created by the Balzan, with the collaboration of the Balzan Prizewinners.

To promote and supervise all these initiatives, two Commissions have been set up, one between the Balzan and the Swiss Academies (at present composed of Thierry Courvoisier and Markus Zürcher) and another between the Balzan and the Lincei (at present composed of Sergio Carrà and Paolo Matthiae). Both commissions are chaired by Alberto Quadrio Curzio as a representative of the Balzan, which is also represented by Enrico Decleva, while the Balzan Secretary General, Suzanne Werder, has been appointed Secretary of both Commissions.

June 2015

THE BALZAN FOUNDATION "PRIZE"

BOARD

(December 2015)

ALBERTO DEVOTO   *Member*
                        Professor in the Physics Department of the
                        University of Cagliari; former Scientific Attaché of
                        the Embassy of Italy in Washington; appointed by
                        an inter-ministerial decree of the Italian Ministry
                        of Foreign Affairs and Ministry of Education,
                        Universities and Research as Representative of the
                        Italian Republic on the Balzan Foundation "Prize"
                        Board

PAOLA GERMANO   *Member*
                        Executive Director of the DREAM programme,
                        Community of Sant'Egidio; PhD in Infectious
                        Diseases at the University La Sapienza, Rome

PAOLO MATTHIAE   *Member*
                        Professor Emeritus of Archaeology and History
                        of Art of the Ancient Near East at the University
                        of Rome "La Sapienza"; Fellow of the Accademia
                        Nazionale dei Lincei, Rome; appointed by
                        the Balzan General Prize Committee as their
                        Representative on the Balzan Foundation "Prize"
                        Board

GENERAL PRIZE COMMITTEE

(December 2015)

SALVATORE VECA	*Chairman* Professor of Political Philosophy at the Institute for Advanced Study (IUSS), Pavia
ENRIC BANDA	*Vice Chairman* Research Professor of Geophysics at the Institute of Earth Sciences in Barcelona, Spanish Council for Scientific Research (CSIC); former Secretary General of the European Science Foundation, Strasbourg; former President of Euroscience, Strasbourg; Member of the Real Academia de Ciencias y Artes, Barcelona
PAOLO MATTHIAE	*Vice Chairman* Professor Emeritus of Archaeology and History of Art of the Ancient Near East at the University of Rome "La Sapienza"; Fellow of the Accademia Nazionale dei Lincei, Rome
ETIENNE GHYS	*Member* Research Director at the Centre National de la Recherche Scientifique, Pure and Applied Mathematics Unit, École Normale Supérieure de Lyon; Member of the Académie des sciences, Institut de France, Paris
H. CHARLES J. GODFRAY	*Member* Hope Professor of Zoology at the University of Oxford and Fellow of Jesus College; Fellow of the Royal Society
BENGT GUSTAFSSON	*Member* Professor Emeritus of Theoretical Astrophysics at the University of Uppsala; Member of the Royal Swedish Academy of Sciences, the Royal Danish Academy of Sciences and Letters, and the Norwegian Academy of Science and Letters

JULES A. HOFFMANN	*Member* Professor at the Institut d'Études Avancées at the University of Strasbourg; former President of the Académie des sciences, Institut de France, Paris; 2011 Nobel Prize for Physiology or Medicine
PETER KUON	*Member* Professor of Romance Philology at the University of Salzburg, Austria
LUCIANO MAIANI	*Member* Professor Emeritus of Theoretical Physics at the University of Rome "La Sapienza"; Fellow of the Accademia Nazionale dei Lincei, Rome, and of the American Physical Society
THOMAS MAISSEN	*Member* Director of the German Historical Institute in Paris; Chair in Early Modern History at the University of Heidelberg; Member of the Heidelberger Akademie der Wissenschaften
ERWIN NEHER	*Member* Professor Emeritus, Max Planck Institute for Biophysical Chemistry, Göttingen; Member of the Academia Europaea; Foreign Associate of the US National Academy of Sciences and of the Royal Society, London; 1991 Nobel Prize for Physiology or Medicine
ANTONIO PADOA SCHIOPPA	*Member* Professor Emeritus of Legal History at the University of Milan; former President of the Istituto Lombardo, Academy of Sciences and the Humanities, Milan; Foreign Fellow of the Académie des inscriptions et belles-lettres, Institut de France, Paris
DOMINIQUE SCHNAPPER	*Member* Research Director at the École des hautes études en sciences sociales (EHESS), Paris; Honorary Member of the French Conseil Constitutionnel; Foreign Fellow of the Accademia Nazionale dei Lincei, Rome

THE BALZAN FOUNDATION "FUND"

BOARD

(December 2015)

ACHILLE CASANOVA
President
Former Vice Chancellor of the Swiss Confederation and spokesman of the Federal Council; former delegation leader of the Consultative Cultural Committee Italy-Switzerland; Ombudsman of the public German-language Swiss radio and television service; appointed by the Swiss Federal Council as Representative of the Swiss Confederation on the Balzan Foundation "Fund" Board

LUISA BÜRKLER-GIUSSANI
Member
Attorney at Law

ENRICO DECLEVA
Member
Former Rector of the State University of Milan; former President of the Conference of Italian University Rectors (CRUI)

ALBERTO DEVOTO
Member
Professor in the Physics Department of the University of Cagliari; former Scientific Attaché of the Embassy of Italy in Washington; appointed by an inter-ministerial decree of the Italian Ministry of Foreign Affairs and Ministry of Education, Universities and Research as Representative of the Italian Republic on the Balzan Foundation "Fund" Board

CLAUDIO GENERALI
Member
Former Member of the Governing Council of the Canton of Ticino, responsible for finances and public works; former President of the Association of Foreign Banks in Switzerland and former Vice President of Swiss Radio and Television RTS; Chairman of the Ticino Banking Association

BALZAN PRIZEWINNERS
FOR LITERATURE, MORAL SCIENCES, AND THE ARTS; FOR PHYSICAL, MATHEMATICAL AND NATURAL SCIENCES, AND MEDICINE

2015

Hans Belting (Germany) History of European Art (1300-1700)

Francis Halzen (Belgium/USA) Astroparticle Physics including neutrino and gamma-ray observation

David Michael Karl (USA) Oceanography

Joel Mokyr (USA/Israel) Economic History

2014

Ian Hacking (Canada) Epistemology and Philosophy of Mind

David Tilman (USA) Basic/applied Plant Ecology

Dennis Sullivan (USA) Mathematics (pure/applied)

Mario Torelli (Italy) Classical Archaeology

2013

Alain Aspect (France) Quantum Information Processing and Communication

Manuel Castells (USA/Catalonia) Sociology

Pascale Cossart (France) Infectious Diseases: basic and clinical aspects

André Vauchez (France) Medieval History

2012

David Charles Baulcombe (UK) Epigenetics

Ronald M. Dworkin (USA) Jurisprudence

Kurt Lambeck (Australia/The Netherlands) Solid Earth Sciences, with emphasis on interdisciplinary research

Reinhard Strohm (UK/Germany) Musicology

2011

Bronislaw Baczko (Switzerland/Poland) Enlightenment Studies

Peter Robert Lamont Brown (USA/Ireland) Ancient History (The Graeco-Roman World)

RUSSELL SCOTT LANDE (UK/USA) Theoretical Biology or Bioinformatics

JOSEPH IVOR SILK (USA/UK) The Early Universe (From the Planck Time to the First Galaxies)

2010

MANFRED BRAUNECK (Germany) The History of Theatre in All Its Aspects

CARLO GINZBURG (Italy) European History (1400-1700)

JACOB PALIS (Brazil) Mathematics (pure and applied)

SHINYA YAMANAKA (Japan) Stem Cells: Biology and Potential Applications

2009

TERENCE CAVE (UK) Literature since 1500

MICHAEL GRÄTZEL (Switzerland/Germany) The Science of New Materials

BRENDA MILNER (Canada/UK) Cognitive Neurosciences

PAOLO ROSSI MONTI (Italy) History of Science

2008

WALLACE S. BROECKER (USA) The Science of Climate Change

MAURIZIO CALVESI (Italy) The Visual Arts since 1700

IAN H. FRAZER (Australia/UK) Preventive Medicine

THOMAS NAGEL (USA/Serbia) Moral Philosophy

2007

ROSALYN HIGGINS (UK) International Law since 1945

SUMIO IIJIMA (Japan) Nanoscience

MICHEL ZINK (France) European Literature (1000-1500)

BRUCE BEUTLER (USA) and JULES HOFFMANN (France/Luxembourg) Innate Immunity

2006

LUDWIG FINSCHER (Germany) History of Western Music since 1600

QUENTIN SKINNER (UK) Political Thought; History and Theory

PAOLO DE BERNARDIS (Italy) and ANDREW LANGE (USA) Observational Astronomy and Astrophysics

ELLIOT MEYEROWITZ (USA) and CHRISTOPHER SOMERVILLE (USA/Canada) Plant Molecular Genetics

2005

PETER HALL (UK) The Social and Cultural History of Cities since the Beginning of the 16th Century

LOTHAR LEDDEROSE (Germany) The History of the Art of Asia

PETER and ROSEMARY GRANT (USA/UK) Population Biology
RUSSELL HEMLEY (USA) and HO-KWANG MAO (USA/China) Mineral
    Physics

2004

PIERRE DELIGNE (USA/Belgium) Mathematics
NIKKI RAGOZIN KEDDIE (USA) The Islamic World from the End of the 19th
    to the End of the 20th Century
MICHAEL MARMOT (UK) Epidemiology
COLIN RENFREW (UK) Prehistoric Archaeology

2003

REINHARD GENZEL (Germany) Infrared Astronomy
ERIC HOBSBAWM (UK/Egypt) European History since 1900
WEN-HSIUNG LI (USA/Taiwan) Genetics and Evolution
SERGE MOSCOVICI (France/Romania) Social Psychology

2002

WALTER JAKOB GEHRING (Switzerland) Developmental Biology
ANTHONY THOMAS GRAFTON (USA) History of the Humanities
XAVIER LE PICHON (France/Vietnam) Geology
DOMINIQUE SCHNAPPER (France) Sociology

2001

JAMES SLOSS ACKERMAN (USA) History of Architecture
JEAN-PIERRE CHANGEUX (France) Cognitive Neurosciences
MARC FUMAROLI (France) Literary History and Criticism (post 1500)
CLAUDE LORIUS (France) Climatology

2000

ILKKA HANSKI (Finland) Ecological Sciences
MICHEL MAYOR (Switzerland) Instrumentation and Techniques in
    Astronomy and Astrophysics
MICHAEL STOLLEIS (Germany) Legal History since 1500
MARTIN LITCHFIELD WEST (UK) Classical Antiquity

1999

LUIGI LUCA CAVALLI-SFORZA (USA/Italy) The Science of Human Origins
JOHN ELLIOTT (UK) History, 1500-1800
MIKHAEL GROMOV (France/Russia) Mathematics
PAUL RICŒUR (France) Philosophy

1998

    HARMON CRAIG (USA) Geochemistry
    ROBERT MCCREDIE MAY (UK/Australia) Biodiversity
    ANDRZEJ WALICKI (USA/Poland) The Cultural and Social History of the
        Slavonic World

1997

    CHARLES COULSTON GILLISPIE (USA) History and Philosophy of Science
    THOMAS WILSON MEADE (UK) Epidemiology
    STANLEY JEYARAJA TAMBIAH (USA/Sri Lanka) Social Sciences: Social
        Anthropology

1996

    ARNO BORST (Germany) History: Medieval Cultures
    ARNT ELIASSEN (Norway) Meteorology
    STANLEY HOFFMANN (France/USA/Austria) Political Science:
        Contemporary International Relations

1995

    YVES BONNEFOY (France) Art History and Art Criticism
    CARLO M. CIPOLLA (Italy) Economic History
    ALAN J. HEEGER (USA) The Science of New Non-Biological Materials

1994

    NORBERTO BOBBIO (Italy) Law and Political Science
    RENÉ COUTEAUX (France) Biology
    FRED HOYLE (UK) and MARTIN SCHWARZSCHILD (USA/Germany)
        Astrophysics

1993

    WOLFGANG H. BERGER (USA/Germany) Palaeontology with special
        reference to Oceanography
    LOTHAR GALL (Germany) History: Societies of the 19th and 20th Centuries
    JEAN LECLANT (France) Art and Archaeology of the Ancient World

1992

    ARMAND BOREL (USA/Switzerland) Mathematics
    GIOVANNI MACCHIA (Italy) History and Criticism of Literature
    EBRAHIM M. SAMBA (Gambia) Preventive Medicine

1991

> György Ligeti (Austria/Hungary/Romania) Music
> Vitorino Magalhães Godinho (Portugal) History: The Emergence of Europe in the 15ᵗʰ and 16ᵗʰ Centuries
> John Maynard Smith (UK) Genetics and Evolution

1990

> Walter Burkert (Switzerland/Germany) The Study of the Ancient World
> James Freeman Gilbert (USA) Geophysics
> Pierre Lalive d'Epinay (Switzerland) Private International Law

1989

> Emmanuel Lévinas (France/Lithuania) Philosophy
> Leo Pardi (Italy) Ethology
> Martin John Rees (UK) High Energy Astrophysics

1988

> Shmuel Noah Eisenstadt (Israel/Poland) Sociology
> René Étiemble (France) Comparative Literature
> Michael Evenari (Israel/France) and Otto Ludwig Lange (Germany) Applied Botany

1987

> Jerome Seymour Bruner (USA) Human Psychology
> Richard W. Southern (UK) Medieval History
> Phillip V. Tobias (South Africa) Physical Anthropology

1986

> Otto Neugebauer (USA/Austria) History of Science
> Roger Revelle (USA) Oceanography/Climatology
> Jean Rivero (France) Basic Human Rights

1985

> Ernst H.J. Gombrich (UK/Austria) History of Western Art
> Jean-Pierre Serre (France) Mathematics

1984

> Jan Hendrik Oort (The Netherlands) Astrophysics
> Jean Starobinski (Switzerland) History and Criticism of Literature
> Sewall Wright (USA) Genetics

1983

    Francesco Gabrieli (Italy) Oriental Studies
    Ernst Mayr (USA/Germany) Zoology
    Edward Shils (USA) Sociology

1982

    Jean-Baptiste Duroselle (France) Social Sciences
    Massimo Pallottino (Italy) Studies of Antiquity
    Kenneth Vivian Thimann (USA/UK) Pure and Applied Botany

1981

    Josef Pieper (Germany) Philosophy
    Paul Reuter (France) International Public Law
    Dan Peter McKenzie, Drummond Hoyle Matthews and Frederick John
        Vine (UK) Geology and Geophysics

1980

    Enrico Bombieri (USA/Italy) Mathematics
    Jorge Luis Borges (Argentina) Philology, Linguistics and Literary
        Criticism
    Hassan Fathy (Egypt) Architecture and Urban Planning

1979

    Torbjörn Caspersson (Sweden) Biology
    Jean Piaget (Switzerland) Social and Political Science
    Ernest Labrousse (France) and Giuseppe Tucci (Italy) History

1962

    Paul Hindemith (Germany) Music
    Andrej Kolmogorov (Russia) Mathematics
    Samuel Eliot Morison (USA) History
    Karl von Frisch (Austria) Biology

BALZAN PRIZEWINNERS
FOR HUMANITY, PEACE AND FRATERNITY
AMONG PEOPLES

2014   Association Vivre en Famille (France), the creation of a maternity unit and the revitalization of a school in Ibambi in the Democratic Republic of the Congo (DRC)

2007   Karlheinz Böhm (Austria/Germany), Organisation *Menschen für Menschen*, Aid for Ethiopia

2004   Community of Sant'Egidio, DREAM programme combating AIDS and malnutrition in Mozambique

2000   Abdul Sattar Edhi (Pakistan/India)

1996   International Committee of the Red Cross, endeavours in the hospitals of Wazir Akbar Khan and Karte Seh in Kabul, Afghanistan

1991   Abbé Pierre (France)

1986   United Nations Refugee Agency

1978   Mother Teresa of Calcutta (India/Macedonia)

1962   H.H. John XXIII (Vatican City/Italy)

1961   Nobel Foundation

FINITO DI STAMPARE
PER CONTO DI LEO S. OLSCHKI EDITORE
PRESSO ABC TIPOGRAFIA • SESTO FIORENTINO (FI)
NEL MESE DI LUGLIO 2016

The Annual Balzan Lecture